The Pseudonomicon

OTHER TITLES FROM FALCON PRESS

By Christopher S. Hyatt, Ph.D.
Undoing Yourself With Energized Meditation
Energized Hypnosis (book, audios and videos)
Radical Undoing: The Complete Course for Undoing Yourself (audios & videos)
The Psychopath's Bible: For the Extreme Individual
Tantra Without Tears
Dogma Daze
To Lie Is Human: Not Getting Caught Is Divine

By Christopher S. Hyatt, Ph.D. with Lon DuQuette & Aleister Crowley
Aleister Crowley's Illustrated Goetia

Edited by Christopher S. Hyatt, Ph.D. with contributions by Wm. S. Burroughs, Timothy Leary, Robert Anton Wilson et al.
Rebels & Devils: The Psychology of Liberation

By S. Jason Black and Christopher S. Hyatt, Ph.D.
Pacts With the Devil: A Chronicle of Sex, Blasphemy & Liberation
Urban Voodoo: A Beginner's Guide to Afro-Caribbean Magic

By Antero Alli
Angel Tech: A Modern Shaman's Guide to Reality Selection
Angel Tech Talk (audios)

By Phil Hine
Condensed Chaos: An Introduction to Chaos Magick
Prime Chaos: Adventures in Chaos Magick

By Peter J. Carroll
PsyberMagick
The Chaos Magick Audios

By Israel Regardie
The Complete Golden Dawn System of Magic
What You Should Know About the Golden Dawn
The Golden Dawn Audios

By Joseph C. Lisiewski, Ph.D.
Israel Regardie & the Philosopher's Stone
Kabbalistic Handbook for the Practicing Magician
Kabbalistic Cycles & the Mastery of Life
Ceremonial Magic and the Power of Evocation

By Steven Heller
Monsters & Magical Sticks: There's No Such Thing As Hypnosis?

**For the latest on availability and pricing
visit our website at http://originalfalcon.com**

The Pseudonomicon

by
Phil Hine

THE *Original* FALCON PRESS
TEMPE, ARIZONA, U.S.A.

International Standard Book Number: 978-1-935150-64-0
ISBN 978-1-61869-640-3 (mobi)
ISBN 978-1-61869-640-0 (epub)
Library of Congress Catalog Card Number: 2004108709

First Edition 1994 Chaos International
Second Edition 1997 Dagon Productions
Third Revised Edition 2004
by special arrangement with Dagon Productions
Fourth Printing 2009

Disclaimer:
It is generally agreed by experienced magicians that working with the Cthulhu Mythos is dangerous due to the high risk of obsession, personality disintegration or infestation by parasitic shells. Whilst giving this opinion due consideration, I have decided to release this material since, before the throne of Azathoth, questions of who is sane and who is mad become inconsequential.

The paper used in this publication meets the minimum requirements of the American National Standard for Permanence of Paper for Printed Library Materials Z39.48-1984

Address all inquiries to:
THE ORIGINAL FALCON PRESS
1753 East Broadway Road #101-277
Tempe, AZ 85282 U.S.A.
(or)
PO Box 3540
Silver Springs, NV 89429 U.S.A.
website: http://www.originalfalcon.com
email: info@originalfalcon.com

TABLE OF CONTENTS

ACKNOWLEDGEMENTS

Fraternal greetings to any fellow former members of the Esoteric Order of Dagon who might happen to peruse this book. My particular thanks go to: Norvegicus, Fra. Areon, IOT Pact USA, Jim Barry, Dave Mitchell, and Maria Strutz.

This book is dedicated to Brother R.B.B and Sor. Sona N'yl. My thanks for their respective inspirations.

Cover chaosphere shows detail from "Yog-Sothoth" by Fra. Shugal 333, EOD.

Insect God artwork, page 49, by Phil Hine.

Artwork and Photos pages 13, 40, 45, 53, 56, 57 by Maria Strutz.

This booklet was first published as a limited edition of 300 by Chaos International, 1994.

INTRODUCTION

Magic is not something that can be confined. It quickly spills out into other life areas, occasionally catching the unwary off guard, propelling the practitioner into a liminal space of heightened sensibility and awareness of other presences, other possibilities. The realisation that "everything is alive and significant," as William S. Burroughs put it, is only a breath away. To enter the faery realm takes but a single step. Magic is not something which one merely 'does.' It's personal, up-close. It twists you and skews your perception of the world, tipping you into a world of signs and portents. A territory of fathomless symbol; of mysteries lurking in the shadows. The magician is hypersensitive to the sudden implosion of significance, which is at times a blessing, and at others, a curse.

How do we gather meaning from this magical world of signs? What makes one experience valid and another not? Despite the claimed empiricism of modern magicians, this is not a rational process. Once we enter the domain of magic, rationality becomes a limited tool, and it's often difficult to communicate to someone else just why an experience is significant, even between those who share similar perspectives. For me, significance is characterised by a degree of *gnosis* or revelation. It is an experience which impels me to action, be it reflection, consideration or the opening up of a new area of exploration. What is important is that it is a personal truth— something that 'feels right.' Which is not to say that it cannot be questioned. It is important to challenge, whilst at the same time cherish such experiences. For the curse of this sensitivity to significance is obsession. It's all too easy for the magician to drown in an ocean of heightened meaning, to the point where every chance encounter is a meeting with an inner-planes adept; where every song lyric has a personal message aimed at you; where every animal is a familiar spirit and all your friends were magicians in a previous incarnation. Everything becomes significant, not merely personally, but also on a cosmic scale. In such ways are fanatics born; those who have stopped enjoying magic, and suffer from it instead.

The fictional territories of H.P. Lovecraft—the haunted hills of Dunwich, the woods of Arkham, the deep ocean and the maze-like urban areas portrayed in "The Horror at Red Hook" or "Pickman's Model"—are replete with a sense of lurking presences, of a hidden sentience which pervades the atmosphere. His descriptions of places and settings combine the precision of dreams with a degree of ambiguity that allows the reader to fill in the gaps, as it were. His protagonists enter these territories as outsiders, only to become gradually (and shockingly) aware of what is hidden there, until the full significance of the reality of the Great Old Ones impacts upon them, changing them forever. They enter a world from which there is no turning back, bowed down by secrets which cannot be shared by others who have not experienced the revelation, or taken fully into the world of the outer beings and their allies.

Lovecraft's lore is a territory of hints and come hithers. The ultimate revelations suffered by his narrators are never clearly stated, the 'forbidden books' found in shadow-shrouded libraries never reveal the truth, leaving only clues and giving rise to more questions. The landscape of signs remains mysterious, and we have to make our own meanings rather than looking them up in a handy reference work.

Thus *The Pseudonomicon*—a jumble of tentative postcards from my own excursions into the Lovecraftian imaginary.

— Phil Hine, 2004

CTHULHU MADNESS

Each god brings its own madness. To know the god—to be accepted by it—to feel its mysteries, well you have to let that madness wash over you, and through you. This isn't in the books of magic, why? For one thing, it's all too easily forgotten, and for another, you have to find it out for yourself. And those who would sanitize magic, whitening out the wildness with explanations borrowed from pop psychology or science—well, madness is something that we still fear—the great taboo. So why did I choose Cthulhu? High Priest of the Great Old Ones. Lying dreaming "death's dream" in the sunken city, forgotten through layers of time and water. It sounds so simple to say that I merely heard his "call"— but I did. Gods do not, generally, have a lot to say, but what they do say, is worth listening to.

I recall one evening staying in a friend's flat. I'd been "working" with Gaia. No new-age mommy with a channeling about saving whales or picking up litter. I felt a pressure inside my head building up—something huge trying to pour itself into me. Sensations of geological time—layers sleeting through my awareness. The heat of magma; slow grinding of continents shifting; the myriad buzz of insects. Nothing remotely human. This sort of experience helps me to clarify my feelings on Cthulhu. Alien but not alien. A vast bulk stirring somewhere around the pit of my stomach. A slow, very slow heartbeat crashing through waves. Lidded eye peeling back through darkness, back through the world, the cities, the people walking outside, peeling back slowly. Peeling back through my entire life, all memories and hopes crashing into this moment. Waking from the dream of this to feel a stirring—a nagging disquiet; the absolute fragility of myself thrust back at me through crashing waves of silence.

This is the sense of Cthulhu madness.

Cut to walking through a forest. It is pouring with rain. The trees are bare of leaves, slimy, mud churning underfoot. I'm seeing them as clutching fingers attempting to snare the sky; as winding tentacles.

9

Cthulhu is all around us. It is a squid-thing, bestial, dragon-winged—a theriomorphic image, but such things are all around us, as trees, insects, plant life, and within us as bacterium, brooding viruses; born momentarily through the alchemical transformations taking place in my body even as I write. Hidden. Dreaming. Carrying on without our cognisance. Unknown beings, with unknown purposes. This thought builds in intensity and it throws me sideways into realisation. That Nature is alien to us. There's no need to look for hidden dimensions, higher planes of existence or lost worlds of myth. It's here, if we but pause to look and feel.

The old Gods are everywhere. Their features outlined in the rock beneath our feet. Their signatures scrawled in the fractal twisting of coastlines. Their thoughts echoing through time, each lightning storm an eruption of neural flashes. I'm so small, and it (Cthulhu) is so vast. That such an insignificant being becomes of the focus of that lidded eye peeling back across aeons of time—well, it puts me in my place, doesn't it. My carefully-nurtured magician-self ("I can command these beings, *I can!*") goes into momentary overdrive and then collapses, exhausted by the inrush of eternity. Run away. Hide.

Having tried to break out of the mould I have only succeeded in breaking down. I scream inwardly for my lost innocence. Suddenly the world is a threatening place. The colours are too bright and I can't trust them anyway. Windows are particularly fascinating, yet they too become objects to be suspicious of You (I) can't trust what comes through windows. We can look out of them, but other things can look in. I press my hand to the glass. What secrets are locked into these thin sheets of matter? I would be like glass if I could, but I'm afraid to.

Sleep brings no respite. The eyelid begins to peel back even before I sleep. I feel as if I'm falling, tipping like a child's top into something...I don't know what. All pretence at being a magician has failed. This thing is too big. I can't banish it and even if I could, I have a strong sense that I mustn't. I have opened this door and unwittingly stepped through it, like walking deliberately into a puddle only to find that I'm suddenly drowning. Cthulhu's pulse-beat echoes slowly around me. Cthulhu is dreaming me. I was unaware of this, and now I am acutely aware of it, and wish to hell I wasn't. I want to sink back into unconsciousness. I don't want to *know* this. I find myself developing rituals of habit. Checking plug sockets for stray outpourings of electricity; avoiding particularly dangerous trees, you know the kind of thing.

I thought I was a rising star, yet I'm reduced to the four walls of my room. But even they won't keep these feelings out. Slowly, some self-preservation mechanism kicks into gear. Madness is *not* an option. I can't stay like this forever—another casualty of what is never mentioned in the books of magic. I begin to pick up the patterns I've let slip—eating regularly (at more or less the right times), having a wash, going out for walks. Talking to people—that kind of thing. I feel the sensation of the lidless eye peering out of abysses of time and memory, and I find I can meet that eye ("I") steadily. The environment ceases to be a threat. The self-protection rituals (obsessions) fall away, and after all, what is there to protect? The dreams change. It is as though I have passed through some kind of membrane. Perhaps I have become glass, after all. The thoughts of Cthulhu stirring down there in the darkness are no longer fearful. I find that I can, after all, ride the dream-pulse. What was that lidless eye but my own "I" mirrored through fear and self-identifications? I'm no longer haunted by strange angles. All resistance has collapsed, and I've found myself a measure of power in its place.

Of course this theme is familiar to one and all—the initiatory journey into and out of darkness. Familiar because of the thousand and one books that chart it, analyse it, and, in some cases, offer signposts along the way. Which brings me back to why I chose Cthulhu, or rather, why we chose each other. There's something very *romantic* about H.P Lovecraft. The same romance which brings people towards magic by reading Dennis Wheatley. As Lionel Snell once wrote *"When occultism dissociated itself from the worst excesses of Dennis Wheatley, it castrated itself for the worst excesses of Dennis Wheatley are where it's at."* There's something gut-wrenching, exciting, awe-ful—romantic—about Lovecraftian magic. Contrast it with the plethora of books available on different magical "systems" which abound in modem bookshops. Symbols everywhere—everything has become a symbol, and somehow, (to my mind at least), less real. Awesome experiences have had all the feeling boiled out of them, into short descriptions and lists—always more lists, charts, and attempts to banish the unknown with explanations, equations, abstract structures for other people to play in.

Lovecraftian magic is *elemental,* it has an *immediate* presence, and resonates with buried fears, longings, aspirations and dreams. The Great Old Ones and their kin can only ever be fragments of the mysterious, never to be codified or dried out for scholars to pick over. Yes, you can bounce gematria around until you've equated this god with that concept, and I do feel that gematria, if used appropriately, can become a thread with which you can begin to weave your own Cthulhu madness, tipping yourself into sub-schizoid significances. There are no Necronomicons—okay, I'll amend that, there are several *published* necronomicons, but none of them for me do justice to that sense of an "utterly blasphemous tome" which sends you insane after a thorough reading. If it does exist, it's in a library somewhere where you will have to go through madness to get the key, only to find that what works for you, probably won't make much sense to everyone else. After all, to some people, *Fanny Hill* was blasphemous. The whole point of the necronomicon is that it is a cipher for that kind of experience which twists your whole worldview and, whilst the insights of that illumination are dancing around your head, impels you to *act* upon it—to do what "must" be done in the fire of *gnosis*—whether it be Dr. Henry Armitage setting forth to Dunwich or Saul's conversion of the Greeks, the flames of his vision on the road to Damascus dancing in his heart. This experience, this core, out of which magis—power—bursts forth, for me is the core of magic—the central *mystery,* if you like. Gnosis of the presence of a god rips away the veils and leaves you gasping, breathless. Character armour is blown away (until it slowly accrues into a shell once more) and briefly, you touch the heart of that unknowable mystery, coming away with a shard embedded. It drops away, it works its way in, it becomes a dull ache, so we have to go back for more. Most of the "set" magical rituals that I've done or participated in don't even come close to this. Yet all the magical acts which I have done, responding to external circumstance, the crash of events or some burdening inner need have thrust me into the foreground of the mystery. I can still remember seeing a witch priestess "possessed" by Hecate. The eyes... weren't human. This year, in answer To my plea out of confusion and torment, the wild god Pasupati stooped down low and peered down at me, a vision of blazing whiteness, the afterburn of which is still glowing at the edges.

Real magic is wild. I can feel the near-presence of the Great Old Ones at night. When the wind rattles the window-panes. When I hear the growl of thunder. When I walk up a hillside and ponder on the age of that place. To feel them near me, all I would have to do is stay there until night fell. Stay away from the habitations of men. Away from our fragile order and rationality and into the wildness of nature, where even the eyes of a sheep can look weird in the moonlight. Outside, you don't need to "call things up"—they're only a breath away. And you are nearer to Cthulhu than you might otherwise think. Again, it's a small thing, and rarely mentioned, but there's a difference between a "magician" thinking he has a right to "summon the Great Old Ones," and a magician who *feels a* sense of kinship with them, and so doesn't have to call. Anyone can call them, but few can do so out of a nodding acquaintance born of kinship. There's a great difference between doing a rite, and having the *right*. But once you've faced a god, letting it's madness wash through you, and change you, then there is a bond which is *true*, beyond all human explanation or rationalisation. We forge bonds with the gods we choose and with the gods which choose us. It's a two-way exchange, the consequences of which might take years to be manifest in your life. But then, gods tend to be patient. Cthulhu dreams.

INVOCATIONS OF OTHERNESS

Why choose to work magically with the Great Old Ones and their kin?

There are several reasons why a magician might find such work of personal value.

Uncharted Territory

Unlike most magical entities, the Mythos of the Old Ones is relatively bare of detail—hence the attempts by some occultists to merge them into identifiable maps of correspondences and symbolism. The stories in which these entities appear in are tantalisingly fragmentary, yet all the key elements of magical exploration are present: a sense of sacred landscape; the power of dreams; participation in the sabbat; scrying; shape-shifting, and more. From the bare bones of the Mythos, a magician can weave himself a uniquely personal "system" based on experience with these entities. It matters little whether or not the nuances of this system can be transmitted to others, as long as it works.

Romantic Glamour

The idea of daring to summon beings of incalculable power who are likely to rip your face off regardless of how well you perform the conjuration has in itself an attraction. It's glamorous, especially if you still harbour the secret wish that magick is, really, like the business that goes on in the horror movies—you know, blonde virgins, ancient altars, things with tentacles responding to your summoning—and let's face it, what magician doesn't? Cthulhu Magick has an attractive glamour because it still retains an aura of mystery and menace about itself—something which has been lessened in other forms of contemporary magick (which has been gnawed at by psychologists, apologists and would-be physicists). Magick should be dangerous, shouldn't it? Playing games with insanity and existential angst comes with the job, as it were. Similarly, Cthulhu Mythos magick can be appealing due to its "git 'ard" status, as opposed to presumably working with Isis, which is generally perceived by some people as "softies magick."

This is a mistaken perception, in my experience. Isis may not have tentacles, but she can be one mean mother. There's nothing particularly wrong with holding such a glamour about the Great Old Ones (or anything else), but it can limit your vision, and narrow your range of options for working with these entities.

The Outsider Stance

This is an attitude of mind which is very much related to the above. It is perfectly in keeping with Lovecraft's basic scenario, since a great many of his narrators were "Outsiders"—people who, by virtue of their forbidden knowledge, genealogy, or interests, stood on the fringes of civilisation. Alternatively, they went out on a limb as a result of their arcane studies. As they crept closer to the unspeakable truth, they retreated beyond the boundaries of rationality and the concerns of ordinary society. Again, this can be a core part of the trip. Fine. I've met any amount of desperately doom-laden young men who seem to be convincing themselves that bohemian decadence can be achieved whilst living in a small room on an even smaller income.

A cynic, however, might look at these "outsiders" and point out that they happen also to be neurotic, repressed (whilst of course, maintaining the opposite), and desperately lack anything which resembles basic social skills. It may not be nice to hear, but unfortunately one of the attractions of the occult for some people is that you can convince yourself that you are a mighty adept whilst everyone else is continually amazed at your total ineptitude on planes more solid than the astral.

The reason I am saying this is because that's what I was like, when I first started doing magick, and became particularly interested in the Cthulhu Mythos entities. It's probably a phase you have to go through, like having zits or something, but of course you get the opportunity to grow out of it.

Antinomianism

Cthulhu Mythos magick can contribute to the development of an Antinomian stance. A core principle of Chaos Magick is that continued deployment of antinomian techniques upon yourself is vital to magical development, hence the various Libers of Crowley, and the stress placed on metamorphosis and liberation in Liber Null, to name but two sources. The criteria for success with this practice is subtle. You can easily spot someone who wears his "weirdness" on his sleeve (often they're trying so hard at it that it has the opposite effect), yet a magician skilled in the antinomian stance doesn't have to make any kind of display. Antinomian practice is commonly associated with the concept of becoming "alien"—something which again has a romantic glamour. But becoming "alien" is much more than a matter of dressing in strange clothes and saying "beep beep" to people (or "Hail Shub-Niggurath," if you prefer). No, look again at the movies and horror-stories. Often, the most successful aliens are the ones who blend into the crowd.

So how does the Cthulhu Mythos assist this process? Firstly, the Great Old Ones are not particularly interested in humanity. Most magically-used entities have some kind of declared interest in humanity, which makes them useful for enchantment, divination, illumination, etc. What use is something that thinks humans are at best, useful insects, and, whose main form of communication is producing a hole in your carpet?

Well, the very fact that they're not interested whatsoever in human aims, desires, and most of the things which we think are important is in itself useful. If you work from this perspective, then of course you are going to see humanity as ants, but it is also likely that you will get a new insight into your own complex of desires, attitudes, and motivations. Now this sort of thing can easily lead to mysticism, which is where you end up if you have misunderstood the kind of aphorism which says that a banquet is equal to a few scraps on the rubbish-heap.

Why so many people choose a life of self-imposed poverty to one of indulgent opulence as a way of being mystic, we may never know. Fortunately, good magicians avoid such a fate.

But there is more to it than metanoia—seeing yourself from a different perspective. A core feature of the Cthulhu Mythos is Transfiguration—evolution into a new mode of being, such as a Deep One or Ghoul. This transfiguration brings not only a new perspective, but also the ability to live in other worlds, and a kind of self-sufficiency that does not depend on other people's views and judgements. This is akin to Spare's principle of Self-Love, which I have examined in some depth in Prime Chaos. The theme of Transfiguration is closely examined later in this book.

Becoming the Beast

Related to both the practice of Antinomianism and Transfiguration is the process of integration with our so-called "Monstrous Souls."

This process has three stages, which might be described as: Fear the Beast; Feel the Beast; Feed the Beast. In practice, this process is akin to entering atavistic states of awareness in order to integrate them within the psyche—under will, as it were. There is a great deal of power in this aspect of the Great Old Ones—the shadowy adumbration's of power which have been long suppressed and denied, that which is beyond the "ordered" universe which we inhabit most of the time. Which is why I so persistently disagree with attempts to mesh the Great Old Ones into existing magical systems—their power lies in the fact that they are "undimensioned and unseen." Likewise, the dark terrors of the psyche retain their power because they can never fully be bound.

You cannot bind them into a triangle—you have to abandon all safety and enter their world. If you return, you will return transformed.

The elements of this three-stage process can be discerned in the works of Kenneth Grant, and more recently, Linda Falorio and Mishlen Linden. The Tunnels of Set are but one route into this twisted Gnosis, and I shall examine other facets in due course.

Earth Rites

The factors which I have discussed above relate to the intrapsychic condition of the magician. However, another factor brought up by working with the Great Old Ones is that of perceptual interaction with Nature.

At first this might sound strange, as the Old Ones are generally thought of as being beyond the natural. However, as Lovecraft writes, "...the wind gibbers with their voices and the earth mutters with their consciousness."

Trying to understand the Old Ones from the perspective of the general western magical tradition is very much akin to that of a scientist trying to grips with natural phenomena. As Benoit Mandelbrot (1984) says:

The existence of these patterns challenges us to study these forms that Euclid leaves aside as being formless, to investigate the morphology of the amorphous. Mathematicians have disdained this challenge, however, and have increasingly chosen to flee from nature by devising theories unrelated to anything we can see or feel.

I feel this view is similar to that of western magick, which has a very "indoors" feel to it. At least, whenever I performed rituals such as the Lesser Banishing of the Pentagram, I have always felt that such procedures are not appropriate for outdoor work. Just as scientists have retreated from the chaotic complexity of nature, in favour of laboratory testing and the search for microscopic particles, so magical theory tends to create an internal Tower of Babel, where symbolism shields the user from direct perception of reality. Mythos magick stands outside the edifice of symbol systems and carefully-constructed hierarchies of spirit. The stress I have placed on deconditioning and antinomianism serves to reduce the tendency to map perception according to conditioned reflexes. Rather, perception becomes an act of sensuous communion with the world we are immersed in. Perception has been traditionally described as a purely passive, internal event, with each sense thought of as separate from the others. This is how perception has been studied, but it does not correlate to our immediate experience of perception, which is global, rather than categorised.

A great deal of magical technique is designed to focus awareness along a single directional vector. The use of sigils, meditational symbols, mantras, etc., help to achieve a state where consciousness of object is lost, and the focus of attention, fueled by gnosis, is projected forth. I have found that, in working Mythos magick, it is useful to develop a reverse talent, the widening of awareness without particular focus, until one perceives all aspects of the immediate environment as a medium for possible communion.

Our perception of the environment does not remain constant. Spend a week or so away from the image-haze of urban life, and you will begin to notice changes in your perception of the immediate environment, particularly if the internal word dialogue is replaced with silence for long periods. "Normal" consciousness of urban life differs markedly from "normal" consciousness of the country. Translate these awareness shifts into your awareness of urban living and you will find new vistas of perception unfolding around and within you. You are bringing perception of the Old Ones back into the city.

Transmutations

One consequence of Cthulhu Magick that has often been proposed is that the magician who aligns himself with this current is actively introducing such elements into the human life-wave. This is a very common idea in magical metaphysics, and most magical orders tend to the view that their work is contributing (in one way or another) to the evolutionary development of human culture. Those who adhere to this view with respect to the Cthulhu Mythos posit the argument that contact with the Old Ones is a process of uniting the chthonic roots of primeval consciousness to the stellar magicks of the future. This idea can be discerned in the magical writings of adepts as distinct as Dion Fortune, Kenneth Grant and Pete Carroll. Below the abyss, this issue is debatable. Above the abyss, it is irrelevant.

THE MYTHOS AND MAGICK

A good deal of my impulse to attempt a work of this nature comes from the dissatisfaction I have felt with other texts which have attempted to translate the Cthulhu Mythos into an operational magical format.

Most texts tend to follow the format of a grimoire—a collection of rituals and spells for the reader to use. However, given the nature of the Cthulhu Mythos, I have never felt that it is entirely appropriate to simply fit existing magical procedures around it. Consequently, when working with the Great Old Ones, I have tended to develop operational procedures which differ from those inherent in the western magical tradition. This seems to me to be in keeping with the atmosphere of the Mythos tales, where the sorceries relating to the Great Old Ones bear more relation to the ecstatic practices of shamanism, witchcraft survivals, or voudoun, rather than the intellectual tradition of the Golden Dawn and its offshoots.

Theory and Application

Much of what passes for magical theory is a hodge-podge of concepts, ranging from theosophy-derived maps of the inner planes to pop psychotherapy and "alternative" physics. The question of how much of it is "True" in the absolute sense is irrelevant, at least from a Chaos perspective, since it is the investment of belief in a concept which makes it viable, rather than its coherence. Most occult theories are treated in the same way as general scientific descriptions of the world. That is, they are presumed to be "true" independently of human experience. These are known as *Theories-of-Action*. However, there is a second type of theory, *Theory-in-Use*, which relates to the guidelines and patterns that a practitioner learns, through practice and individual experience, which enable him to be effective.

I find this distinction between formalized and personal concepts to be particularly useful when approaching the Cthulhu Mythos. Theories-in-use cannot be taught: they are personal and tend to operate at the level of unconscious assumptions. They can only be learned by the individual by a process of practice in "live" experience. In the same way, magical theories-in-use cannot be taught. A fledgling magician can be given theories-of-action and taught basic techniques and application of them, but he must develop his own theories-of-use as part of the process of becoming an Adept. In these terms, an Adept would be the magician whose personal theories-in-use have been honed to the point where he no longer requires any set formulations or theories.

I have found that working with the Cthulhu Mythos entities is very much a personal process, and so much so that I do not feel that it is appropriate to give out set formulations for rituals and the like.

Instead, I will examine some of the magical techniques which are particularly appropriate for Cthulhu Mythos work, but it is up to you as to when and how you apply them.

On Banishing

The ubiquitous 'Banishing Ritual' is generally considered a key element of standard approaches to ritual magic. So much so, that it is often automatically assumed that every ritual event should begin with some kind of banishing ritual. In other words, it becomes a habit, the use of which is not questioned. The concept of the Banishing Ritual seems to have originated with the Hermetic Order of the Golden Dawn, and gone on to permeate most post-Nineteenth Century approaches to magic, from the various 'traditions of Wicca to Chaos Magic. In order to discuss the relevance of Banishing Rituals to Cthulhu Magic I will pose the question, what is a Banishing Ritual for? Again, the answers to this will depend very much on individual taste, but here are two common 'explanations' for the usage of banishing rituals:

"The ritual creates a fortified and cleansed physical/astral space which is a vital precondition for any formal magical act—be it meditation or further works of ritual."

"It prevents the magician being attacked by malevolent forces."

Generally, a Banishing Ritual consists of the willed re-ordering and sacralisation of space, according to a particular schema or structure. The user establishes herself at the centre, or *axis mundi*, around which are arranged at least 4 cardinal points or directions with some symbol of aspiration or transcendence (godhead, Tao, Chaos) 'above' the user. The cardinal points become stations at which may be traced protective symbols such as pentagrams, or at which may be invoked protective spirits such as archangels, god or goddess forms, etc. Banishing Ritual scripts tend to follow a pattern whereby the user, by means of speech, movement and visualisation, makes connections between their self, physical space, and astral space. This is generally held to not only create a 'safe' space as a preliminary for further magical work, but to help the magician make the demarcation between ordinary behaviour and thinking, and focusing on the magical activity that they are about to do.

Just as a Banishing is generally performed to open a formal magical event, it is also used to 'close' an event, acting to shut down the 'magical space' and reinforce the 'ending' of the ritual event and the return to ordinary consciousness. Generally then, the banishing ritual is concerned with establishing boundaries—either to keep unwanted influences out, or, in some cases, for establishing a space for inviting presences *in*. Further, the banishing ritual acts as a formalised demarcation of the movement from 'ordinary' space and consciousness to 'magical' space and consciousness. The act of doing a banishing helps the individual take on the role of being a magician, and helps her focus her mind onto the magical acts she is about to undertake, leaving aside the cares and concerns of her day-to-day existence.

Underlying the general use of banishing rituals there seems to be an assumption that magical events can only take place within a specially prepared space—almost to the extent that magic can only occur within such a space and cannot otherwise intrude into one's daily experience, as though magical experience can be turned on or off at will. Indeed, classical authors of the western esoteric tradition have made much of the injunction not to allow magical levels of experience to intrude into one's day-to-day consciousness. The banishing ritual reinforces the distinction between mundane (day-to-day) reality and magical reality. This distinction is not an absolute—it stems from a particularly western intellectual tradition and there may well come a point in one's magical work when it no longer tallies with one's personal experience of magical reality.

This latter point is significant in terms of Cthulhu Mythos magic. In Lovecraft's stories, the Great Old Ones and their kin are ever-present. His sorcerers and cultists go to dark and lonely places where their presence can be felt. He continually stresses the point that once opened, the door swings both ways. The infamous Simon Necronomicon presents the rather melodramatic warning that "there are no effective banishings for the forces invoked in the NECRONOMICON." Some occult critics of Cthulhu magic appear to take this literally, whilst others have rightly, to my mind, exposed it as a prime example of magical 'hype.' For me, the issue is not so much that Cthulhuoid entities cannot be banished, but whether the concept of banishing itself is useful when approaching the magical landscape that Lovecraft has bequeathed us.

Alternatives to Banishing

The first point to consider is that banishing is *contextual*. There may be situations when it is entirely appropriate to begin and end a magical event with a formal banishing ritual, and others when it is not. One can only make this kind of distinction through practical experience.

Secondly, it can be useful to distinguish between the two modes of banishing—*opening* and *closing*. Once this is done, then it becomes easier to consider alternative approaches to formal ritual structures. For opening a magical event, we might consider other approaches to acknowledging moments of transition. A simple, yet often effective approach for indoor workings is to make transitions using changes in light. Moving from electric lighting to darkness, and then to candle or fire-light can itself create a subtle shift in mood. Another simple approach is the use of sound. A magical event begins in silence, into which gradually creeps the sound of a flute, gong, or singing bowl. Simple methods such as these can do a great deal to build an atmosphere of tension and heightened expectation on the part of celebrants, which is entirely appropriate to opening a magical event. In outdoor workings, sound can be particularly effective, especially if it is some distance away from the immediate site. For solo practitioners, developing patterns of silent movement & gesture can be useful (Steve Wilson's 1994 book, *Chaos Ritual* gives some excellent exercises for devising personalised postures, gestures, etc.) alternatives to more formal rituals.

Events as opposed to rituals

For the present discussion, I'd like to draw the reader's attention to the distinction between magical *rituals* and magical *events*. The term "ritual" usually implies some degree of formal structure, scripting or sequencing of distinct elements (even if the ritual is enacted on an *ad hoc* basis). Rituals have distinct beginnings and endings. Magical events however, can be a lot more 'fuzzy' around the edges. Whilst rituals are usually intentional activities, events need not be, and can include those odd, spontaneous situations wherein the uncanny intrudes into everyday life without those present necessarily having to do anything intentional. Thus a 'magical event' may be triggered by a ritual or some other intentional magical act, or conversely, a magical event may lead the participant(s) to enact a ritual in response to it. A magical event can encompass a great deal more than a particular ritual or its immediate consequences. Sometimes, it is only in retrospect that we can pinpoint the 'trigger' of a magical event. Talking about magical events rather than rituals allows us to consider those elements of magical experience that create context and meaning. All too often, rituals are presented as distinct 'scripts' which are devoid of any background—much in the way that a cookery recipe is presented, but with less attention to the result. Personally, I find it much more interesting to read about a ritual within the creators' or users' personal context—what led them to create or attempt the ritual, their observations on it, how they felt afterwards, followed by any long-term consequences or other results.

Magical events can also include intentional acts that are not formal rituals, yet undeniably have an effect on the participants.

Orchestrating events

When attempting to orchestrate any kind of magical event, I feel it is important to take into account the kind of emotions and sensations that are appropriate to it. Just by tone of voice alone, you can raise in yourself (and any others present) a sense of expectancy or imply an ending to an event. Speaking in a hushed tone and speaking in a firm, authoritative voice carry different messages. In amongst the nebulous discussions of symbolism and magical energies, it's easy to forget that even a formal banishing ritual is a synthesis of movement, gesture, and speech, and that these are just as important, if not more so, than the symbolic elements.

Achieving closure

Achieving the *closure* of a magical event is often more difficult than opening one. Using formal banishing and circle-closing ritual structures tends to give rise to the belief that once these have been performed, the magic 'stops' and all participants are 'back to normal.' However, from my experience of doing magical work both as an individual and in various groups over the last twenty-odd years, I have to say that things are rarely so simple. Recovery, or "coming down" from an intense magical event may be a lengthy process. I have participated in rituals which have been 'closed' by a formal banishing and the ritual leaders have assumed that everything was 'back to normal' even when some participants were clearly not yet recovered from the intense state of consciousness which the ritual helped them achieve. When you think about it, this is not so strange. Magical work can thrust practitioners into intense states of consciousness, occasionally culminating in intense visions, revelations, and life-changing experiences. So perhaps it would be useful to distinguish between *immediate* closure and *long-term* closure. Immediate closure is the demarcation made to signify the ending of a magical event—what one does to wind down, in other words. This can range from gestures and declarations of closure to taking down any props or trappings used, writing immediate perceptions of the event in a diary, discussing the event with fellow participants, etc. Long-term closure is more related to dealing with the effects that the magical event has had on you. Participating in a magical event is rather like going to a good movie or play. It transports us into another realm. When the lights go up and the curtain comes down, the immediate event is over, but we leave that magical space with the feelings & thoughts that it has evoked in us. If we go with friends, the event may continue as it is discussed, dissected, and favourite moments shared and re-lived. Sound bites get used in conversation, provoking laughter and reconnection. A magical event may also do this. Indeed, for me, a measure of success for a magical event is that it brings forth new ideas, new connections between concepts, a sense of reconnection with the world. So long-term closure is for me concerned with the personal integration and assimilation of the effects of the ritual into my life at a day-to-day level. Of course how one does this is more amorphous and of necessity, going to be different for each individual. In my own experience, there have been occasions where formal banishing sequences did not seem, at the time, to be appropriate, and equally, others when formal ritual banishings have not been sufficient in themselves, to achieve closure.

With respect to Cthulhu Magic, how one approaches both opening and closure will depend to a large extent on what the intent and aims of a particular magical event are. For example, a magical event orchestrated with the intent of promoting both individual and group dream-contacts with Great Cthulhu opened with a reading of the Lovecraft story, the *Call of Cthulhu*, after which the group walked in silence along a beach, listening to the pounding of the waves, reflecting on the power and vastness of the ocean, and what mysteries lay beneath it. Upon reach a rocky promontory, one member of the group led the others through a guided visualization sequence, after which the group walked back along the beach, collecting pebbles, paddling in the water, discussing striking rock formations. At no point during this event were there any formal 'banishings' done because the intent of the event was for group members to retain the 'atmosphere' of the ocean, to promote a sense of connection with Cthulhu and the deep ocean, and thus be able to evoke memories of the event prior to sleep, in order to try and stimulate dreams of Cthulhu. This event was little more than telling a story in an appropriate setting, which can be just as 'magical' (if not more so) as formal rituals.

A couple of years ago, I was present at a Cthulhu magic ritual (itself part of a series of workings) during which one of the other participants became convinced that some alien entity had entered the temple space and was wandering around 'loose' as it were. This led to a rather heated discussion about the pros and cons of how to close the ritual. Some participants were of the opinion that some kind of formal banishing *should* be performed, else we risk said entity turning up and bothering people outside of the ritual, whilst others (and I must own up to being in the latter camp) opined that it might be interesting if said entity *did* turn up outside of the agreed ritual hours. Eventually, someone of neither persuasion pointed out that the argument itself had probably done more to effectively dispel any lingering sense of magical atmosphere and that once the lights went up and the ritual props were taken down, then a round of drinks and some level-headed debate might be all that was necessary. Since we were working in a more-or-less permanent temple, then the space itself did not really need 'closing,' but it was further suggested that those who did wish to close themselves off from any lingering ritual ambience could do so in their own way, and that perhaps those of us who wanted to maintain that possibility of something weird coming a-calling, could equally do something to maintain that vital connection or perhaps even enhance it.

There is a good deal of magical apocrypha—tales of interpersonal mayhem and downright weirdness—ending with the punchline—"Well, he/she/they didn't banish properly, you see." One of the most common types of storyline, and one which comes up a great deal in respect to Cthulhuoid magics is that of the practitioner behaving oddly or apparently 'going mad' for a period, the cause of which it seems popular to lay at the door of either the fact that person(s) in question were experimenting with the Cthulhu Mythos, and/or that they didn't banish 'properly.' I've heard this said about various individuals by third parties, and even on occasion, by those concerned themselves. In my opinion, it's too easy to make pat comments about either 'not banishing' or whether one magical system or another can lead to 'madness' or not. When it comes down to it, the practice of magic leads to change (otherwise, why do it?), and it has to be admitted that change is not always (indeed, IMO, it's not usually) as it's often portrayed to be, the gradual move towards 'higher' states of consciousness and degrees of superior holier-than-thou-ness. Even the most lemon-scented new age niceness can do your head in, if you're up for it. The underlying issue, for me, is not that we can periodically find ourselves behaving like assholes, but that we take responsibility for doing so after the fact, rather than blaming it on the magical work we were doing, be it alone, or with other people. Trying to do otherwise, is tantamount to saying "god (insert appropriate entity) made me/us do it."

The Liminal Gnosis

I use this term to group the magical techniques used for willed dreaming, scrying, astral (virtual) explorations and the like. Liminal Gnosis can be loosely described as a passive state of consciousness where the magician allows thoughts, images, sounds, visions, etc. to well up before him. This state can be accessed, for example, by lying down and relaxing after physical exertion. Part of the trick here is not to attempt to direct the visions that arise, but to relax into them and let a thread of cohesion emerge organically. Alternatively, by imagining the image of a particular location, such as Kadath in the Cold Waste or the Monastery of Leng, this state can be used to trigger dream or astral journeys. This state also extends to the perception of strange sounds, fleeting presence's seen at the corner of one's eye, etc. Entry into the Liminal Gnosis can be deliberate (i.e., formalized), although the magician may find himself slipping into such a state of awareness as a result of the hidden combination of perception and association. The key to this state is to learn to recognize the different routes into it, and then use it appropriately.

In Mythos fiction, Lovecraft stresses that use of scrying surfaces, dreaming etc., to enter the realm of the Old Ones is a two-way gateway. Just as you may enter through such gates, so others may seek egress through them. In Mythos magick, this is likely to happen, particularly if mirrors are used as gateways, and it may happen that an image that is evoked into a mirror will seem to leave it and enter your working space. Reports of such occurrences turn up in the magical records of Dee and Crowley, for example.

Methods of Dream Control

One of the simplest approaches to Dream Control is to use a graphic or mantric sigil, prior to sleeping. Reading a Cthulhu Mythos tale can also be effective, as can vividly imagining some particular Mythos location, such as Kadath in the Cold Waste. Obviously, keeping a Dream Diary is essential to this kind of work. The use of linked association with scent can also produce evocative dreams. If you can link a particular experience (such as a waking astral descent to R'Lyeh) with a particular scent, then if this scent is evaporated on an oil fragrancer by one's bedside, this can also trigger controlled dreaming.

Sigils, images, and magical objects found in dreams can also be used, in order to try and explore them further. If you have a particularly interesting dream-sequence, try using it as a conscious pathworking performed on the edge of sleep—you may find that the sequence is continued as you dream.

Emotional Engineering

States of fear, neurosis and borderline paranoia can occur regularly throughout Cthulhu Mythos work. Indeed, I would recognize such reactions as a sign of success in getting to grips with this region of magical experience. However, these states can get out of hand. When stripped of cognitive associations and projected fantasies, fear becomes an excitatory gnosis, and paranoia a state of heightened perception.

I would say that it is useful then, to be familiar with processes that allow you to experience emotions as bodily sensations, while stilling the cognitive element when necessary. The Ego-deconstructive practices given in *Liber Null*, for example, are useful in this respect.

One of the simplest methods of deconstructing emotional states is as follows:

a) When you find yourself in the grip of a powerful emotion, do not attempt to suppress it, but allow yourself to be fully absorbed into it.

b) Be aware of what sensations there are in your body as the emotion intensifies.

c) By an effort of will, still the internal dialogue's tendency to cycle through past events which brought on these feelings, and future events which tend to be projected as fantasies.

d) Be aware of the bodily sensation, and continue to still any thoughts which tend to identify this sensation as one particular emotion or feeling.

e) The resultant state of awareness can then be used for magical work, such as entry into the Liminal Gnosis.

Shape-Shifting

Shape-shifting is a recurrent theme throughout the Mythos stories. It usually takes the form of transition from a human to quasi-human form, such as the transformation into a Deep One. Shape-shifting can be useful in astral explorations and in working through the "Becoming the Beast" process I outlined earlier. See the section entitled *Transfigurations* for more on this theme.

Generally, the practice of Shape-Shifting can be done either as a form of meditation or by using excitatory trance. In the former, the magician both visualizes his body outline changing and uses kinaesthetic memory to "feel" a change in posture and centre of gravity. In the latter, the trance takes the form of a violent possession of the zoomorphic shape required, and should be preceded by techniques such as wild dancing, seething, or group ritual.

Glossolalia

The use of strange words of power, barbaric names and twisted languages is also a recurrent theme in Mythos fiction. The rapid delivery of vowel/consonant sets at random (glossolalia) can be used to develop a route to gnosis which can climax as possession by "nameless" masks which speak in word-bursts. If such an exercise is prefaced by a particular intention, then you develop your own power-words for a wide variety of use and application.

One example of this technique in Mythos magick is to enter trance via any preferred method and seek to meld your awareness with a specific facet of the Great Old Ones—not so much identification with one "name" or another, but what lies beyond that name, and, as you slip into that altered perception, begin glossolalia and continue until a sound-burst evolves. Emerging primal mantras can be vibrated in a wide variety of ways, from staccato hissing, to a deep rumbling from the stomach. Experiment and find your own power mantras to evoke routes into the gnosis of the Old Ones.

Sorcery

The techniques of enchantment for direct results do not tend to be of primary significance in Mythos magick, since the Great Old Ones have little interest in human desires and motivations. However, techniques for the creation of fetish images, totems and magical weapons are useful occasionally, if you wish to surround yourself with physical representations of the alchemical process of identification with the outer voids. Having said this, I occasionally use R'Lyeh as a "transmission point" for sending sigilized desires outward as a telepathic ripple, and on one occasion became possessed by Tsathoggua during a healing ceremony. So the Mythos magick is not entirely devoid of sorcerous application, but is generally less so than other paradigms.

Obsessive Fetishes

The creation and collection of personal fetishes, artworks and devices aids the process of embedding the Mythos awareness, and many magicians who have worked with these entities have produced images and magical objects which convey aspects of experience which do not translate into words easily. A Mythos fetish need not be, however, a clay representation of Cthulhu, for example, but any object or item which becomes associated with a resonant state of consciousness. Some years ago I possessed a crystal pendulum which was suspended from a metal retort stand.

During one phase of Mythos work, I came to identify the stirrings of the pendulum with the onset of a liminal gnosis which for me, heralded the sense of "nearness" of the Old Ones. This particular state was also heralded with a rising fear of glass window-panes. In such a state, everyday objects or sounds (such as the ticking of a clock) become loaded with a kind of global significance.

Into this classification also fall peculiar states of oracular perception, as distinct from the deliberate use of divination techniques. Again, it is very much the case that one is swept into these states—a collision with oracular time which may be triggered by events in the environment—the patterns glimpsed as flocks of starlings whirl between buildings; the meaning arising from the movement of traffic; the distant creaking of an iron gate. Much depends on the state of consciousness of the magician, and this will be explored further in the section entitled *Purposive Disintegration*.

Frenzy

Although many of the magical techniques alluded to in Lovecraft's work are generally that of the solo magician, such as scrying, dreaming, etc., Lovecraft also made mention of Frenzied Rites reminiscent of witchcraft or voudoun, in Lovecraft's mind "degenerate" orgies by which cultists summoned the Old Ones. This reminds us of the power of the physical forms of gnosis: drumming, chanting, flagellation, dancing, and the abandonment of sexual taboos and self-restraint. Such extremes are common in mythic history, such as the Bacchanalia, or the archetypal witches' sabbat. Such cultic activities celebrate the primal power of the Old Ones, and can be used as forms of communion, wherein the "walls" between order and chaos are momentarily dissolved, and all sense of self is negated in the timeless rhythms of ecstatic frenzy.

The construction of such "Free Areas" is rare in western magick, where total abandonment is extremely difficult to achieve, particularly in a group setting, where spontaneity and abandonment tend to clash with the linear sequencing of most ritual arrangements. There have been a few experiments in ordered group work arising from chaotic flow, but this area requires more work. A combination of whirling, low-frequency strobe lights, tape-effects, masks, and sudden shifts in the pace of "ritual flow" have been found useful here. The sense of unpredictability can be heightened if, in group ritual, not all celebrants know what to expect during the ceremony. Judicial use of mood-altering chemognosis may also be helpful.

Sexual Magick

The use of specialized techniques of sexual magick in respect to the Mythos can be found within the works of Kenneth Grant. One of the commonest forms of sexual gnosis which can be applied in Mythos magick is the facilitation of altered states of consciousness brought on by sexual arousal, which can be used as a springboard for exploration of astral or dream zones. The use of sexual gnosis to charge obsessive fetishes is also an obvious application, as is the breakdown of taboos and revulsion's by exploring sexual gnosis outside of one's immediate references. The possible use of group orgia is noted above, although it should be noted that deliberate attempts to orchestrate orgiastic rites rarely succeed, as it depends on the relative abilities of those present to abandon themselves. The combination of slow sexual arousal and restraint can be used to allow a subject to attain a degree of Liminal Gnosis for him or her to enter astral zones, and bring information back to other celebrants. Needless to say, the use of such techniques requires a good deal of experience and trust on the part of all concerned.

THE GREAT OLD ONES

The Cthulhu Mythos displays a recurrent mythic theme; that the "titanic" forces of creation and destruction—the Great Old Ones—have been cast forth from the earth and "forgotten" by civilised humanity and its narrow, materialistic vision. However, whilst they may be forgotten, they are at the same time ever-present, lurking at the frontiers of order, in places where the wild power of nature can be felt. They are chaotic, in the same way that Nature is chaotic, and they retain their primal power since they cannot be "explained" (i.e. bound) or anthropomorphized. They exist outside linear, sequential time, at the border of "Newton's sleep."

In *Prime Chaos* I gave some cursory descriptions of the major entities of the group known collectively as the Great Old Ones. Separating the Old Ones into distinct entities can be of some use when working with them, particularly for the formation of distinct practices and cults. However, for this present work, I will consider Azathoth, Yog-Sothoth and Nyarlathotep as separate parameters of a single, conterminous entity. Indeed, the term "entity" is in itself misleading, in this respect.

The Great Old Ones, collectively, can best be described as a fractal surface that is continually seething and changing. If you look at a fractal form, you will discern clear patterns and shapes which arise from the surface. The relationship between the Old Ones as distinct entities and their overall existence, is similar to that of patterns in the fractal landscape. Their shapes, forms, and identities arise out of our interaction with them at any given point. We might well call this fractal surface "Nature's Chaos" as it forever lurks on the borders of our artificial, linear experience of the world, and the Old Ones, as we know, have a direct link in the Mythos to storms, earthquakes, and other natural phenomena. In wild places, where nature's chaos is more apparent than the rules of society, the presence of the Old Ones may be perceived. This was well-appreciated by the Ancient Greeks, for example, who designated such frontier places as sacred to the wild gods who might well visit terror or transfiguration upon those who strayed into them. Similarly, the presence of the Old Ones can be felt within, as one enters the appropriate states of consciousness for stepping through into their realm. Such forms of willed madness will be dealt with shortly. The reader will note that this section covers but a few of the aspects of the Great Old Ones—there are obviously others, but they await personal discovery and understanding.

YOG-SOTHOTH

Yog-Sothoth is best approached via a key passage in *The Dunwich Horror* which describes it thus:

> Yog-Sothoth knows the gate. Yog-Sothoth is the gate. Yog-Sothoth is key and guardian of the gate. Past, present, future; all are one in Yog-Sothoth. He knows where the Old Ones broke through of old, and where they shall break through again...."

We know, from the Mythos stories, that the Old Ones have a close relationship with wild places, particularly stone circles, and strange manifestations.

In an earlier essay dealing with Yog-Sothoth I attempted to explore, amongst other things, the understanding of this entity in terms of Earth Mysteries research into light-form phenomena—the Earth Lights hypothesis of Paul Devereaux and others. In researching accounts of strange encounters, ranging from ghosts to UFOs to light-forms, I found that not only were strange sounds a common factor, but also time-sense distortion, pungent odours, and strange visions. Peculiar perceptual shifts appear to occur across a wide range of "encounter" phenomena. During this research, I conceptualized Yog-Sothoth as a kind of "guide" entity for entering states of consciousness appropriate for working with the Old Ones.

However, more recent contacts have modified this viewpoint. From a series of workings (and I use that term rather loosely) conducted with one Fra. Abbadon (by Gematria, 63), formerly of the Esoteric Order of Dagon, I have come to understand Yog-Sothoth less in terms of a distinct entity at the magician's beck and call, but as the "outer edge" of an experience into which the magician progressively slips.

Thus Yog-Sothoth can be described as the outer edge (or the mathematical basis, if you like) of the fractal surface which is the Great Old Ones in toto. Again, this can be understood in the "Beast" process mentioned earlier. "Fearing the Beast" is the response of the magician's sense of boundaries—the Ego prior to the deconstructive work of antinomianism. However, this fear is not merely a defence against the Outer spaces. If purged of attachments, and experienced as pure bodily sensation without identification, fear becomes simply an excitatory gnosis which, if sunk into (as depicted in the image of The Hanged Man), becomes an altered state of consciousness useful for further exploration. This occurs in the form of "Feeling the Beast"—primarily through a type of sensuous gnosis involving the more primitive areas of the brain, resulting in strange kinaesthetic manifestations, "astral" sounds, and the sense of proximity to something vast, yet shadowy.

"Feeling the Beast" is a process of recognition—recognition of both bodily gnosis and higher-order mental images which indicate immersion within the "realm" of the Old Ones. The final stage, that of "Feed the Beast" is a deliberate process known as "the Feast of Yog-Sothoth," wherein the magician is "eaten" by the experience, and thereby achieves full consciousness of the Old Ones.

This process is analogous to the mysteries of Babalon in Thelemic Magick, the Feast of Kali in vama marg Tantra, and the role of Choronzon in Kenneth Grant's elucidation of the Typhonian Current. During this process, the veil of fear from which humanity protects itself against "otherness" is lost, and the by-product is Self-Love and the flowering of what Spare called "supersensuality."

To summarize, then, Yog-Sothoth is the outer edge of experience of the Great Old Ones. Once the magician has successfully melded himself with this edge, he becomes himself a gateway.

AZATHOTH

Azathoth is vaguely described in terms of "a blind idiot god" or a "monstrous, nuclear chaos, the Lord of all things." This gives rise to the image of something which continually, mindlessly, gives rise to chaotic fluctuations and forms. During a working designed to interface with it using via possession (The Mass of Chaos "A"—see *Liber Kaos*). I have heard it described as having an outer "skin" which is a seething mass of "mad souls." It has also been claimed that Azathoth projects and gathers to itself all forms of obsessional thought-forms. This would perhaps suggest that Azathoth performs some kind of Logoic function, endlessly replicating and rearranging forms and structures. In terms of the Fractal surface analogy, Azathoth is that which churns the surface, forming shapes and patterns. In another sense, it can be understood as the whirling void which appears as the dominant ego-persona is progressively deconstructed. The image of Azathoth recalls the danger of identification with one particular persona over another—obsession which may rapidly become megalomania. This also recalls Crowley's image of the "Black Brothers" in *The Vision and the Voice*.

The problem of mania as a result of magical work at any stage of initiation is well-documented, and the fate of those who do not heed warnings about this very real danger is usually a downhill slide into disintegration as the magician strives to maintain an ego-image which is widely at variance with the facts of his existence.

Azathoth may also be understood as the "eye" of Chaos. Lovers of Gematria will find this symbolism replete with imagery for exploration. It's "blindness" recalls both the symbolism of *Liber AL* (c1, v60), and also the technique of turning the senses inward (retroversion of the senses). In Azathoth there is an initiatory trial not to become bound up with one thing or another, else we suffer the fate of the "mad souls" which are its skin. Again, Azathoth becomes a particular experience into which the magician thrusts himself, rather than a distinct entity as the term is commonly used.

NYARLATHOTEP

In the Cthulhu Mythos, Nyarlathotep is distinguished by its appearance of having intelligence, and interest in human affairs. This entity has been variously identified as the "black man" of the archetypal witches' sabbat, as a form of Choronzon-Shugal "the howling guardian," and it also bears more than a passing resemblance to Crowley's description of Aiwass. In the Mythos, Nyarlathotep is both described as "the crawling chaos" and "the messenger and soul" of the Great Old Ones. In the Mythos tales, Nyarlathotep tends to play three roles: that of an Initiator into the Dark mysteries of the Outer gulf; a Nemesis-like agent of destruction, and that of a source of malevolent confusion for the unwary.

My initial approach to Nyarlathotep was, as with the other Great Old Ones, one rooted in traditional magical practice. Nyarlathotep, of all the Great Old Ones, appears on the surface to be a suitable form for invocation, particularly via rites of possession. Experiments in this type of working however, merely served to confirm Nyarlathotep's ability to mislead and obfuscate, and the entity proved to be as cunning and twisted as a Goetic demon. Turning once more to Lovecraft's fiction as a source, I found it more suitable to seek contact with Nyarlathotep through dreaming—where he presides over the astral sabbat, or guardian of various dream-gates such as the Monastery of Leng.

Prolonged work with this aspect of the Old Ones has thrown up two particular perspectives on Nyarlathotep. A great deal depends on how it is viewed (as a qabalist might say, from below, or above the Abyss). Firstly, Nyarlathotep clearly is linked to the Gnosis (knowledge) of the Great Old Ones. This gnosis may be attained through dream or delirium, or even arise unbidden in those who seem to display a natural resonance with this kind of work. The theme of an "initiator" is central to most forms of contemporary magick, and such initiators are often known to be capricious and misleading. Nyarlathotep clearly is a "gateway," a means of ingress, into the gnosis of the Great Old Ones. That it appears malevolent and misleading is unsurprising, given the "blindness" of human thought-processes. Its chaotic presence threatens the carefully-guarded security of the rigid ego, and its insistence on duality (the Aristotelian either/ or) and linear consciousness. Its appearance as bloated and "monstrous" shapes recalls the tendency of the mind to spawn obsessions and then relinquish control to them. Nyarlathotep, in this sense, encapsulates that stage of the initiatory process by which the magician becomes (often painfully) aware of self-erected boundaries and blockages—the borders of his "Achievable Reality."

The second aspect of Nyarlathotep is that of the completed Adept, the magician who has, himself, become a gateway to the Old Ones. In *Liber Kaos*, Pete Carroll describes the Octarine Gnosis (following Terry Pratchett's concept of "Octarine" as the "eighth colour of magic") as relating to the development of the "magician-self," the characteristics of which are:

...antinomianism and deviousness, with a predilection for deviousness and the bizarre.... The magician self, therefore, takes an interest in everything that does not exist, or should not exist, according to ordinary consensus reality. To the magician self, nothing is unnatural.

The magician-self is an invocation of future otherness—in this sense, the magician becomes an avatar of Nyarlathotep through continual practice and development; the process of deconstructing (stripping away) all barriers and boundaries. It is important to note, however, that mere identification with any mental image of Nyarlathotep will not achieve this state, any more than becoming obsessed with the image of Aleister Crowley will allow you to become the Beast 666. Crowley himself discusses the appropriate technique in terms of the magician reducing himself to a void—allowing the "genius" to play through him as it will.

GREAT CTHULHU

In the Mythos stories, particularly The Call of Cthulhu and The Dunwich Horror, Cthulhu is distinguished from the Great Old Ones as their "High Priest" and "their cousin, yet can he spy them only dimly."

He lies, in the sunken city of R'Lyeh "in death's dream" until "the stars are right" for the Old Ones to reclaim the world.

It is significant that the stirrings of Cthulhu send telepathic ripples around the world, bringing waves of disturbance—visions, nightmares, mental breakdown—and causing artists to produce strange images whilst in a dream-like state. Cthulhu is depicted as a zoomorphic form, a vast bulk which has vast wings, and an octopoid head.

Revelation through dreaming is a strongly recurrent theme throughout the Cthulhu Mythos, and it is well known that Lovecraft gained much of his inspiration from his dreams. Cthulhu is generally understood as being "the Lord of Dreams," and is entombed by the city of R'Lyeh in the deep ocean. He is analogous to the chaotic perceptions and desires which have been sealed (or become latent) within the subconscious mind. Elsewhere, it has been said that "we are the dreams and we shall wake them [the Old Ones]." In these terms, Cthulhu/R'Lyeh are a "buried" link within human memory to the gnosis of the Great Old Ones.

Again, the Cthulhu/R'Lyeh image bears all the hallmarks of an initiatory state. This particular gateway is under the deep ocean, a wild territory also under the aegis of Pan. Cthulhu/R'Lyeh transmit currents into humanity, and those who have "heard the call" are inexorably drawn into the depths—revelation and the summons to initiation draws the would-be magician away from consensus reality. The deep ocean is often represented as chaos, or the underworld (Amenta). This analogy is further reinforced if the "sinking" of R'Lyeh is read as a variation on the myth of the "Fall." The image of Cthulhu is reminiscent of many ancient god-forms who have since become demonized—Set, Medusa, Typhon, Hanuman, etc. Zoomorphic entities such as these recall the sense of "participation mystique" which has been lost with the gradual development of the individual ego. Cthulhu can be thus seen as another access-point into beast-consciousness, via the process identified by Austin Osman Spare as Atavistic Resurgence.

As an extension of the above, R'Lyeh can be considered to be an extrusion of Cthulhu, in the same way that a spider extrudes a web. R'Lyeh also partakes of a strange geometry, which, when astrally explored, constantly shift and warp so that tunnels and pathways collapse and overlap each other. This description will surely be familiar to anyone who has worked the Tunnels of Set—and R'Lyeh itself can be considered as a form of this experience. A recurring image from negotiating the paths of R'Lyeh is that they connect "both the dark earth and the stars."

SHUB-NIGGURATH

Shub-Niggurath, the black goat of the woods with a thousand young, is never encountered directly, though it is alluded to in fragments of spells and invocations. Consequently, this particular form of the Old Ones has received little attention, though the suggestion has been made that Shub-Niggurath represents a primal form of Pan. It may be that Shub-Niggurath is an encapsulation of the terror of wild places, such as forests or mountain country. The embodiment of fecundity and tangled growth, Shub-Niggurath could be treated as a bloated genius loci of any wild place; a teratoma emerging from the fleeting perceptions and images which arise when spending a lonely night in some wild place.

Obviously, such "spirits" will have different forms and names, and it is the task of the magician to seek these out and, if possible, enter into a rapport with them.

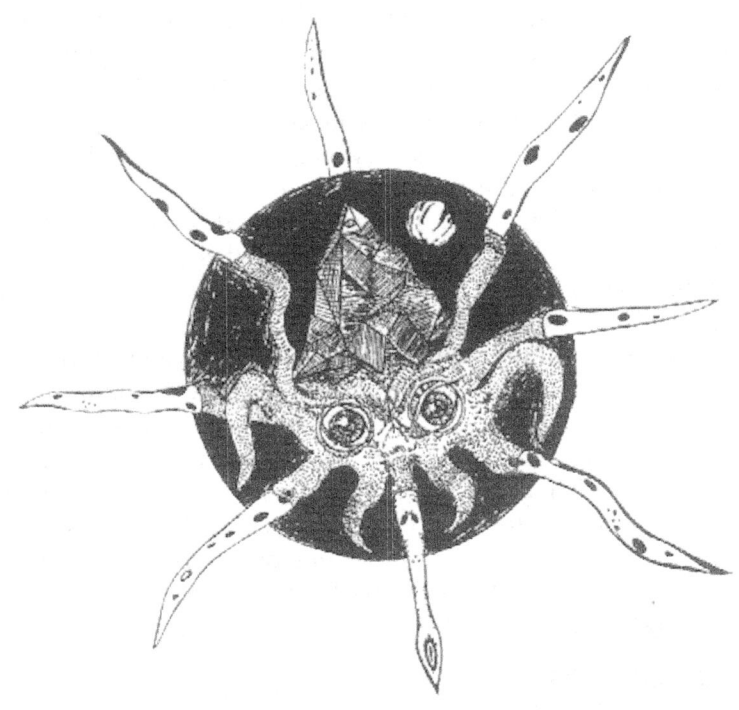

TRANSFIGURATIONS

A recurrent theme throughout the Cthulhu Mythos cycle of stories is that of Transformation from humanity to a zoomorphic form, examples being the aquatic Deep Ones (*The Shadow Over Innsmouth*) and the transition from human to the necrophagic Ghoul (*Pickman's Model*; *The Dream-Quest of Unknown Kadath*).

Such transfigurations are related to dark ancestry or an affinity which draws the subject away from human society into the twilight worlds of the monsters which lurk on the edge of rationality. There is the implication that this process is a direct consequence of entering the realm of the Great Old Ones. Again, this transfiguration calls to mind an initiatory process which appears in myths of human-beast transformation world-wide. An underlying theme is that of transgression, which can be seen in examples of this process such as the Greek myth of Lykanon and the exile of Gwydion and Gilvaethwy in Celtic Myth.

In the magick of the Old Ones, the theme of transfiguration is very much related to the initiation of the outside spaces. In "Becoming the Beast," the magician is deconstructing the boundaries of his ego, and stepping back from his cultural conditioning; at the same time, acknowledging the atavistic desires and complexes which have become characterised as "evil" or "animal" by society.

From the perspective of practical magical work, zoomorphic transformation can be enacted on a number of levels. Firstly, we may consider shape-shifting as a distinct technique for the exploration of astral spaces or for trance-induced sensory and kinaesthetic experience. Shape-shifting into monstrous forms can be used to explore, for example, the bizarre geometries of R'Lyeh or other dream-landscapes.

Secondly, there is the possibility of initiatory ritual. Rites such as the Tibetan "Feast of the Demons" are ritual feints at psychic dismemberment, where the celebrant offers himself up to be ripped apart by his own demonic complexes, in order to be re-born. Such experiences are common throughout magical and shamanic practice, and may often occur spontaneously during an initiatory crisis. Rituals which involve a close proximity to corpses are common in Tibetan and vama marg Tantra, and elements of ritual cannibalism (so repugnant to the modern mind) can be found in most ancient cultures, at one time or another.

The Ghoul's Feast

The Ghoul's Feast is a variant of the above. It may be enacted from a number of different perspectives, but the basic format is that of spending a night alone in the wilderness, and offering one's body as a sacrifice to the Ghouls. Covering parts of one's body in animal offal may be repugnant, but reinforces the sense of sacrifice. None of the usual magical trapping, such as a circle, are necessary, as the stance is one of complete helplessness before the ghouls. The rite may take place partially on an astral level, with the celebrant offering himself as the sacrifice for the ghouls to consume, or the role of the ghouls may be carried out by other celebrants. Consumption is not merely that of the imagined physical body, but also of the ego-complex. Thus the advantage of having other participants who can thoroughly dismember the celebrants' sense of self-importance and worth using tactics such as mockery. The rite appears to climax with the transformation of the celebrant's status from human to one of the company of ghouls. This "passage" may be marked by the celebrant rolling (or being rolled) in mud or excrement, sharing the feast of offal (particularly the brain) or engaging in copulation with another celebrant who has the appearance of a corpse (necrophilic undertones were often present in Asian forms of this rite). The effect of the feast may be intensified by judicious use of chemognosis.

Undercurrent in such a ritual is the idea of relinquishing control to others, and of facing one's own taboos and desires in a way that means they cannot be dodged or evaded. Obviously, the key to such workings lies not so much in how or where to enact them, but when.

Getting the Fear

A key to understanding this type of initiatory experience is that they bring with them varying degrees of Fear. This is fairly explicit in accounts of Initiations, especially when individuals do not know what is going on. This is also true when anything in which we have invested a good deal of emotional commitment and self-esteem is directly threatened or removed suddenly—ranging from emotional patterns to major aspects of life such as career, partner, or dominant self-image. Especially if circumstances are such that we can do little about what is happening. And the character of such initiations does seem to require that our current repertoire of coping strategies are rendered useless. If nothing seems to work, then it might be better to do nothing. But by this I do not mean lapsing into inertia, but assessing the situation and making it an opportunity for change and adaptation.

Fear is very much a bodily gnosis—it tends to reinforce any mental/emotional patterns that serve to keep change at bay. it tends to get channelled into a variety of defence mechanisms, which, while they are not in themselves dysfunctional, can be inappropriate. Fear is basically an excitatory state—the fight/flight reflex of the autonomic nervous system kicking into gear. By deconstructing Fear, we can reconfigure it (when appropriate) into pleasurable excitement, which can be used to fuel movement over a threshold rather than reinforcing patterns which keep it at bay.

Relax into Fear

Again, this is a very old concept. There is a Tantric idea that you can reorient yourself to life so that you are sufficiently open to the avenues of possibilities each moment of living offers, experiencing the world from a condition of "receptive wonder." Related to this is the idea of "Meeting the Guru." Not so much meeting a little old wizened mystic at a bus stop, but knowing that any life event can be the "guru"-teacher, that can spin you sideways into Gnosis and Illumination. There is a similar idea encapsulated within the classical image of the great god Pan. An early depiction of Pan shows him hurling himself (with intent to rape) upon a young goatherd. This image calls to mind the relationship between fear and desire, repulsion and eroticism. Aeneas Tacitus's Polioketika contains several accounts of the effects of Panic-terror as a sudden and unpredictable condition. Philippe Borgeaud, in his book *The Cult of Pan in Ancient Greece* (Chicago Press, 1988), makes the point that Pan "typically attacks a model of order and disrupts it." One of the underlying themes in the classical mythos of Pan is the possibility of creative derangement, of moving from one state to another. Whether this state is one of madness or divine-led inspiration depends on which side of the threshold you view it from. The threat of Pan is ever-present, and he can leap on you anytime, any place—as William Burroughs says, *the sudden realization that everything is alive and significant* (Dead City Radio).

Relaxation into Fear allows self-modification. Here, Fear is not a weakness, but a strength. Allowing yourself to be vulnerable to the forces of Change, particularly the possibility of surprises. Often, the onset of a cross-roads experience throws us into mental entropy—the mental confusion which Pan brings, which pushes us back into bodily sensation. This is a good time to still the mind and attend to sensations—loose the bonds of the past and quiet the mental chaos of "what ifs" and "buts"—cease fantasy projections and sink into bodily sensation. Transform fear into wonder and prepare for new possibilities.

Transform fear into fuel, and examine those patterns which maintained your thresholds. This can become an ecstatic process—the original meaning of ecstasy is "away from stillness," which indicates some measure of agitation. Again, a key to this process is the ability to be "loose" and relaxed. Holding yourself rigid impedes the possibility of entering into new experiences.

I could get up from writing this essay, go into the next room and enact an "initiation" ritual based on a mythic sequence, but myths are merely signposts—the enactment of mythic events is not necessarily the same as undergoing a trial as an Authentic experience. Mythic Initiations can, however, provide a conceptual framework for approaching Experience—an awareness of the dynamics of that process—but they are not the same as living that process. So a ritual act of dismemberment that is Willed may not be as powerful as dismemberment that is experienced as a Crisis. Again, recognition that one is entering a significant crisis-point is possibly more useful than trying to force it to happen.

If you recognise that you are entering a cross-roads, then magical work can be done to maximise the change-potential of that cross-roads. Hence, the success of initiations such as the Ghoul's Feast very much depend on the inner state of the celebrant. As noted above, the brew of fear and desire, when mixed together, can produce powerful intrapsychic reactions. Any working which heightens such reactions via exposure to taboo areas of experience can have immensely powerful consequences, of which one of the most important is a conscious severing of previously-held beliefs and attitudes. The image of the night-stalking Ghoul, eater of corpses and offal, can be seen as the encapsulation of the magician who no longer rejects any part of his experience; who seeks gnosis in all forms whilst being no longer "attached" to anything. As Pete Carroll puts it in Liber Null: *"The most powerful minds cling to the fewest fixed principles."*

PURPOSIVE DISINTEGRATION

A developing theme in this book is that prolonged work with the Great Old Ones imbues the magician with particular states of awareness into which one gradually slips as part of the process of communion. I have described such states as forms of deliberate incursions into borderline mania. In this section, I will explore this process in more detail.

Loss of sanity as a result of being drawn into the realm of the Old Ones is a recurrent theme in the Cthulhu Mythos stories. The narrator often fears for his sanity as he unwillingly accepts shocking "truths" which are revealed as the story builds to its climax. Lovecraft continually reminds the reader that the gnosis of the Great Old Ones is a one-way trip. Once you've entered it, there is no return, at least not in a form that is recognisable. Again, this recalls the initiatory process which, once begun, develops a momentum of its own. At times, the magician may find himself struggling with fear; a refusal to accept inevitable change and the consequences of his flight to the edge of consensus reality. Also common is the problem of mania as a result of gnosis.

It should be recognised that initiation is a process. Each magician may come to recognise his own cycle of peaks, troughs and plateaux. Given time, one may also learn to recognise the aura of onset—the signs that one is tipping into a new awareness. Magical work does strange things to the neurochemical complex. Strange bodily sensations, perceptions and warped concepts of identity are all part of the course, and may be interpreted as psychic attacks or the movement of subtle energies into chakras and so forth. In time, one learns to identify feelings with impeding changes in awareness, developing a finely-tuned oracular awareness of what is about to burst inwards.

In the course of working with the Mythos entities, strange perceptions and ideation's shift through the cracks of linear perception; bubbles which at first are faintly disturbing, yet which may suddenly loom threateningly with an obsessive fervour. Odd suspicions begin to gather.

Everyday of objects such as furniture, glass jars on a shelf, clocks or house plants become imbued with a power and purpose of their very own. Have you ever wondered what your hands do when you are not watching them? Half-seen shapes flicker at the corners of your eyes.

The key to survival when such states creep upon you is to be there fully, yet at the same time dispassionately catalogue them. Be like the "hero" in Cronenberg's remake of *The Fly,* dispassionately cataloguing the disintegration of your being. You may find yourself drawn into personal ritual behaviours which have nothing in common with magical theories or practice. The need to touch a particular spot before you can go to sleep is an unconscious manifestation of anxiety. Anxiety can be understood as fear of loss of control. Relinquish the need to maintain control and feel the trembling in your hands.

Old-time favourites for neurochemical alchemy suggest themselves: fasting, radical alterations in diet, sleeplessness, solitude. Linear consciousness breaks down and all that remains is half-glimpsed and vague. Pretensions to megalomania and self-identification as one thing or another are as illusory as the carefully-constructed facade of consensus reality. Madness and sanity become irrelevant fictions; escape routes that have no permanence.

I realize that this might not come across terribly well. I'm attempting to look back into the years of my own madness and pull out splinters of meaning. Once you've been there, though, you can remember, and by taking on the thoughts and behaviours—almost a process of cut-ups of personal history, the experience of borderline paranoia or disintegration can be replayed. It may start as a form of acting, but do it well and you will invoke your old demons and jerk, puppet-like, to their urges. I remember explaining to a roomful of people my horror—very much coloured by the horror of not being able to communicate that sensation—of sunlight shining through a pane of glass. The disconnected explanation was punctuated by facial twitches, jerking motions of the hands, and sharp rocking movements. Whilst in the grip of demons summoned from my past, I could perceive the reality of the Old Ones directly, and communicate that perception to the others, albeit unsuccessfully.

Once the bright self shatters, many others may arise to fill the vacuum. In time however, all masks become of equal value. Any other identifications, from Higher Self to Dark Genius, become at best temporary formulations, none of which have other than equal prominence. Under the Night of Pan, there is only darkness. It may stop, but it never ends. Occultists writing about Lovecraft often point out that he drew back from the brink of the abyss, and well he might. But there will come at time when drawing back is not an option, just as seeking refuge in one stable self-identification or another no longer becomes viable. The fear of madness only remains tangible when one has a coherent picture of madness. Dump the concept of madness and open yourself to sensation and you may find yourself somewhere quite different.

Such states are sometimes known as initiatory sickness. Much has been made of the similarity between the shamanic initiation and the complex of behaviours known as schizophrenia. Read enough R.D Laing and you may well be able to mimic some aspects of schizophrenic gnosis. I have seen individuals diagnosed as schizo-phrenic attempt to communicate their world-view through a salad of disconnected phrases and numbers, not unlike some of the magical communications from so-called "inner plane adepti." You can almost, but never quite grasp the meaning there, at least not until you have entered the appropriate gnosis. While the schizophrenic indi-vidual may never reach equilibrium within his shattered reality, the magician (at least for some of the time) must do so, to be effective in the world. Therefore court madness now and let whatever remains afterwards go forth.

Unsanity, like magick, sex, and smoking a pipe, is something you have to know intimately to see the benefits of. Suffice to say it remains one of the most powerful taboo areas of modern culture and, for that fact alone, worth a look. I cannot really see the point of any magical approach which does not, at some point, risk derangement. Of course, the whole point is to cross the thin line again and again, until you make no difference between one state and another. From this point, one's will is uncluttered by restrictive images and you are free to let your mad thoughts out and have them work for you as you will.

The gnosis of the Great Old Ones is particularly relevant here. Since human concepts of good and evil, sanity and insanity and many of the driving imperatives such as "Being Right," "Getting Even" etc., have no meaning, working with the Old Ones will enable you to quickly discard them.

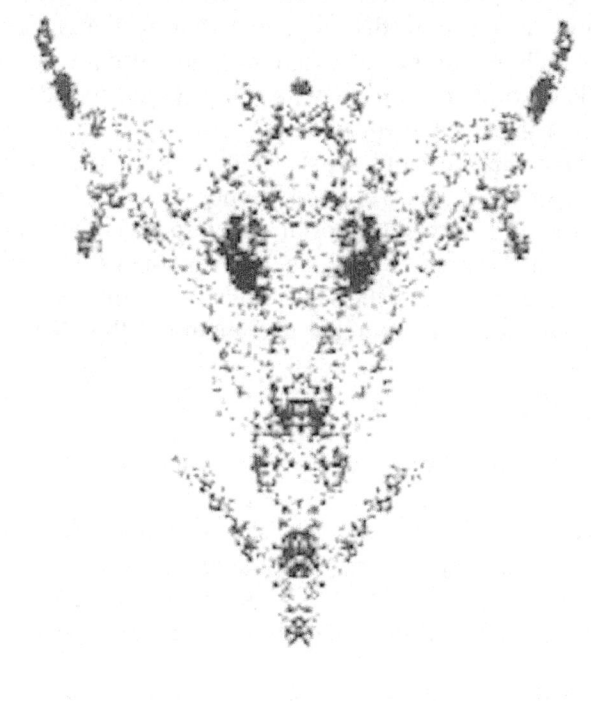

NIGHTLANDS

One of the most common routes into the gnosis of the Great Old Ones is through dreaming and astral vision. In Mythos tales such as *The Dream-Quest of Unknown Kadath,* Lovecraft created the idea of a "Dreamland" (with more than a passing nod to the works of Lord Dunsany) which could be accessed by the intrepid seeker. This dreamland had points of contact with the physical world, and could be used to access places of forbidden mystery such as the Monastery of Leng, Kadath in the Cold Waste, and some of the outer planets where the Great Old Ones were worshipped. Lovecraft's Dreamland seems to partake of a sense of nostalgia, coupled with brooding fear of what lurks at the borders of consciousness. Thus, elements of an idealized past, fantasy, and the fear of what lies unseen on the borders of this space, serve to create and maintain this virtual dreamscape.

The Astral Sabbat

The astral sabbat may be entered via dreams, or use of the Liminal Gnosis. As noted earlier, this is the archetypal witches' sabbat, presided over by Nyarlathotep as the initiator into the mysteries—the Man In Black. It is not unusual for magicians seeking to enter the mythic reality of the Great Old Ones to have spontaneous dreams of attending the sabbat, and these should be taken as a positive indicator.

Larval elemental and zoomorphic entities are very much in evidence, as are forms on the theme of succubi and incubi. The location of the Sabbat tends to be in a wild spot associated with the domain of the Old Ones, such as an underground cavern or forest clearing. Once contact has been made with the sabbat, it is possible to visit it in astral form (human or otherwise) and make more willed interactions with its non-human celebrants. Such interactions should be made from the perspective of freedom of action within the dream, and the magician should not allow himself to become too distracted by the delights offered by elemental entities. Qabalists tend to attribute the Sabbat to the realm of Yesod, and there is a certain degree of fascination (and thereby deception) in the activity therein. One approach to working with the Sabbat experience is to note down all experiences and, with subsequent attendance, to watch out for recurrent themes and consistency of details over time.

The astral Sabbat may be used as a starting point for willed exploration into the dreamland of the Cthulhu Mythos. If you establish any particular sites as related to your work, then these might well appear in your dreamlands. Often, the borderline between waking and dream experience seems to become blurred.

Astral Books

One of the most infamous Magical grimoires of recent memory is Lovecraft's *Necronomicon,* a book which, having escaped from the library of Dream, has appeared in different editions, each purporting to be the "real" thing. However, much of the power of tomes such as the Necronomicon come from their mythic nature. Part of the glamour attached to them is that one hopes to find them in the depths of some dusty shop, and certainly not in the general occult section of a large modern bookstore.

However, the idea of "astral books," encountered in dreams, is well-known to occultists—examples being unwritten books by Crowley and other well-known magi. The general concept is that of access to information through dream or vision. The book is most commonly seen as a repository of knowledge and who knows, in a hundred year's time, its place might have been taken by that of the interactive CD. For the present, however, a recurrent dream-image where forbidden lore may be encountered is the astral library, where the books themselves may be considered sentient.

The "earthing" of astral books is obviously related to phenomena such as automatic writing, channelling, or information received whilst possessed by an entity given over to verbosity of one sort or another.

This kind of communication is very popular in some forms of esotericism, and is often received as new forms of "truth" which those involved feel obliged to spread to the rest of humanity, often through the medium of a vanity press. The majority of such communications tend to reflect the concerns and beliefs of the medium through which they are received. An initial communication of this type might have a high quotient of "new" information, but generally, over time and increased contact, the information level tends to degenerate into psychobabble and rather obvious assumptions.

The recovery of information from astral books such as The Necronomicon can be seen as a form of communication with information which lies at the "edge" of the magician's personal psychocosm. I personally view this type of information-retrieval as a process of meshing new information-gestalts whilst in a state of gnosis. However, if you find the process more glamorous by interpreting it as contact with "outer" states of consciousness, the "dark genius," or the Holy Guardian Angel, then so be it. The information received tends to be consistent with whatever belief system is being used to interpret magical experience—for example, those of a Thelemic persuasion will tend to find that the Necronomicon's data is consistent with Thelemic metaphysics.

Magical dreaming remains one of the more useful techniques open to those who wish to explore the power of the Cthulhu Mythos. The use of sigils, dreamscaping (see *Prime Chaos*), and other techniques can be used to establish a beach-head of astral space which can be used to weave the appropriate psychocosm. There is a definite link between dreams and emotional arousal relating to the Mythos, particularly the borderline states associated with heightened perception and paranoia.

With time and practice, you will find it possible to explore many areas of both the Lovecraftian Mythos and your own personal nightlands using techniques of dream-control.

DARK ZONES

A key element in understanding the power of the Great Old Ones is their relationship to landscapes. Lovecraft makes it clear, through his fiction, that the Great Old Ones manifest into our world through "gateways," and that these gateways are often in wild, lonely places. Places which are entangled with local myth and folklore, which are associated with strange lights, subterranean noises, stone circles and ancient ruins. There are other gateways too—strange angles, subterranean tunnels, wells, and the gates of dreaming, trance, and madness.

The power of such places is ancient and enduring. These are places where we might encounter anything, ghosts, spectral hounds, lost cities, UFOs, or forgotten gods. Such wild places can be found at all points in mythic history. They are areas where the veil between the worlds are at their thinnest, where those who tread the path are at the mercy of terrible forces, and must protect themselves with ritual precautions and proprietary sacrifices. Many of Lovecraft's Mythos tales deal with the gulf of understanding between the urbane, rational city-dweller who crosses into such a dark zone, and the debased myths of the indigenous country-folk, whose tangled lore has at its centre, terror. This theme also recurs through history. The Greeks, for example, associated wild places with the power of Pan, bringer of panic terror. Those who strayed into these areas risked disappearance, transfiguration or death at the hands of supernatural forces.

The Great Old Ones are alien to human civilisation and rationality. Accordingly, suitable power spots for communing with them should carry across this sense of wildness, of brooding power. Such places need not be located far from the haunts of men. Subterranean tunnels—disused mineshafts, abandoned power stations and the like can also carry this sense of timeless brooding. John Keel, in his book *Strange Creatures from Time & Space*, examines the case of West Virginia's "Mothman," whose appearances centred around an abandoned WWII ammunition dump.

Such places are woven about with myth and dread. Any event occurring within such a locality adds to its power, whether it be a battle, murder, or rape. The gestalt of such a site—the encapsulation of its ecology (terrain, plants, animal movements, seasonal changes, atmosphere, history, myth and evolving story) and the consciousness of those who enter its space—is commonly known as the Genius Loci (spirit of place). Just as some spaces seem to have a palpable aura of calm and peacefulness, others transmit a subtle atmosphere, which one might interpret as unwelcoming, or even hatred towards those who enter its borders.

In approaching a possible place of power, it is most useful to cast your senses widely. The most useful thing you can do, initially, is keep quiet and listen. Take note of your surroundings. Visit the site at different times, and if possible, spend a night there. Approach it as you would a powerful person or animal—respect it and take time to get to know it. Fledgling magicians sometimes make the mistake of trying to "raise power" at such a site. If it is, indeed, a place of power, you cannot control it. The approach, rather, is to mesh yourself within it—to become part of it. To find a gate and enter it is not a matter of ritual form, but of entering a state of consciousness—slipping into a state where you can perceive the Old Ones as ever-present.

This state is akin to the lore of Lovecraft's degenerate country folk—the knowledge and awareness that the Old Ones lurk at the edges of civilisation; that at particular times and places, or in the minds of those who have made themselves alien to human concerns, they may enter fully into our world as emissaries of Chaos and Old Night.

Gateways

Of course, there are other forms of Gateway which can be entered. Examples of these include pictures (such as those painted by Austin Osman Spare), angle webs, crystals, scrying mirrors, and a state of consciousness described by Lovecraft which is characterized by an intense sense of nostalgia for that which has long vanished. A place can stir up such a strong sensation without obvious reason, as can a painting, or an arrangement of patterns. This hyper-nostalgia is directionless. That is, it is a longing for something which, while lost, remains unknowable. If this state is maintained over time, without any attempt to focus it in any direction, it becomes a global sensation of moving within a realm of shadows; a turning away from linear consciousness into that which is far more tenuous and chaotic—the Great Old Ones.

APPENDICES

There follow two accounts of the use of Cthulhu Mythos imagery in practical magical work. Firstly, a pathworking which can be used for the transmission of sigilized desire; and secondly, an account of a healing working using the entity known as Tsathoggua.

CTHULHU PATHWORKING

Introduction

This Pathworking uses Cthulhu Mythos imagery to generate conditions for enchantment via Sigils. Here, Cthulhu is defined in its function as the "lord of dreams," based on the Lovecraft tale "The Call of Cthulhu," which relates that, when Cthulhu stirs, "in death's dream," a telepathic ripple is sent across the world. This Pathworking has been used for sending forth "telepathic" communications across a wide area. A sigil should be prepared prior to beginning this working.

Sequence

Begin by having participants relax by any preferred method. The narrative unfolds as a sequence of images:

"All around you is darkness...you hear, on the edge of your awareness, the lapping of waves against a shore. You are standing on a beach.

The sky above is black-blue, tinged with purple. Behind the clouds, you catch faint glimpses of the full moon; a sickly yellow colour.

You walk towards the water, feeling the grains of sand against the soles of your feet. You enter the water—a sudden shock of the cold water against your ankles.

You walk into the water, feeling the cold slowly inching up your body—against your thighs, against your stomach, against your chest.

You continue to walk further into the water, feeling the waves softly lapping against your body, until the water reaches your neck.

For a moment, you hesitate—you have a strange urge to go deeper, but this human body cannot go further. You must change into a form more suitable.

[Note: the form for change can be left open for each participant to decide—suggested forms include a Deep One, or a Shoggoth. In this PW, the form of a Deep One was used.]

You will yourself to change into a creature of the deeps. Webs of skin form between your fingers and toes. Your eyes bulge from their sockets and your mouth widens—you see that your companions are becoming Deep Ones—half human, half frog. You feel lines of gills growing out from your neck. Take a deep breath in—and duck your head underwater (participants hold their breath). You feel a brief spasm of fear, the panic that you will drown, but you open your mouth and exhale, and let the water rush into your lungs. You find that you can breathe easily, though the water at first tastes bitter and salty.

You look around you, finding that you can see easily under water—an eerie blue-green world, fading into the blackness of a deep abyss.

You draw a deep breath, somersault downwards, and swim towards the deeps, moving easily and powerfully, using your new arms and legs.

Down you swim, passing shoals of brightly-coloured fish, into the deep silence of the abyss. As you swim, you become aware of a faint, phosphorescent glow coming from below. You move ever downwards, feeling that somewhere, in the depths below, something awaits you.

Faintly, you now begin to see the dim outlines of mountains or buildings.

As you draw closer, you can see cyclopean blocks of stone, glowing with a faint, greenish light. There are buildings, but you cannot see them too clearly. The angles are wrong—the perspective continually shifts. You are swimming down towards a gigantic city of pillars, towers, of gaping doors and windows; crumbling statues wreathed in seaweed and barnacles. Dimly, you sense a pulsing, throbbing sensation through the water, like the slow beating of a mighty heart.

You are swimming now, over the city—in the distance you can see a vast shape rising before you. As you move closer, you see it is a titanic, black monolith. You pause, and know that this monolith crowns the crypt of Cthulhu—Lord of Dreams. The sigil comes into your mind. You breathe in, seeing the sigil glow in front of your eyes—pause—and breathe out, hurling the sigil against the surface of the monolith. For a split-second it glows against the surface, and then fades out.

Suddenly, from the city, there is a dull rumble, as though an earthquake is beginning. You are caught up by a huge wave of energy, surging up from the below, there is a brief glimpse of crazily tilting angles and planes, and then you are carried back to the surface. There is a moment of total blackness, and then you are lying in the surf, gasping, back in your human shape. Another moment of blackness, and you are back in the temple.

Old Toad Under A Mountain

This is a short account of a working involving Tsathoggua, the protean Toad-entity referred to in Mythos fiction such as The Seven Geases by Clark Ashton Smith.

A couple of years ago I was doing some protracted healing work with a friend, who suffered from swollen glands in the neck. During a trance-investigation of her "psychic body," I "saw" the psychic root of the problem as a toad that had bloated itself up so that it was lodged in her neck.

I was informed, by a familiar spirit, that the only thing that would dislodge this toad was an even bigger toad, and following meditation and divination, decided to invoke Tsathoggua upon myself, following due preparation.

Taking on the aspect of, and drawing upon the power of, Tsathoggua would, I reasoned at the time, enable me to command the sickness-spirit toad to depart from the place wherein it had lodged itself.

I prepared for this working with sleep deprivation and fasting, combined with energetic dancing (to drumming) at a stage event the previous evening. The Rite took place at my friends' house. I drew around us a circle using drum, rattle, bells and free-form chants. I

60

covered my face with white facial paint, ash, and blood. I used a meticulously-knotted series of cords with which to bind my friend, whispering spells of binding into the knots as I twisted them.

The Invocation: I began by visualising Tsathoggua squatting in semi-darkness upon its throne, and then oozing through near-black tunnels and hopping lumberingly between the pillars of a ruined city. I began to move about the ritual space, "feeling" my body outlines as though I were a huge, blundering toad-being; shifting my centre of balance and muttering identifications with Tsathoggua which became increasingly guttural and glutinous. I began to experience those peculiar shifts in consciousness which herald the onset of partial possession; I found that I salivated copiously; that I could feel my tongue swelling to fill my mouth; that my legs refused to bear me upright, and that I could no longer oppose my thumbs, nor could I see clearly through the blur of black and white haze that swam before my eyes. I was, for brief moments, submerged in toad-ness, and then returned, mixing nausea and agony with a thrilling exultation. As I ceased to struggle against the possession, I experienced a curious disengagement. It was as though part of me was standing at one side, observing the entire spectacle, and directing the body that stumbled about the room, moving clumsily to the signals pulsing from the reptilian backbrain.

In this bifurcation of awareness, I saw the big toad and the little toad, crouching in the bound body on the floor. Then I was fully in my own body again, and dragged it over to my friend.

Clumsily opening her mouth, I mentally projected my/Tsathoggua's tongue sliding down her throat, engulfing the lesser entity lodged there, returning, and…gulp! The sickness-spirit was swallowed in my own belly. This act broke the spell. A wave of nausea washed over me and I collapsed, shedding the Toad-skin and metamorphosing from beast-self to human-self, using one of my magical "masks" as a focus for my efforts. After centering myself, I released my friend, banished the area, and continued with a less extreme form of trancework.

Following the working, I slept for a straight 10 hours or so, only to awaken with severe stomach cramps which soon progressed to vomiting. Evidently the "poisons" of the toad-spirit did not agree with me! The nausea lasted about three days before disappearing, and indeed this sort of after-effect from "ingesting" sickness-spirits is not unusual, in my experience.

Comments

1. The relationship between Mythos Entities and the "dragon brain" or limbic system has already been commented upon—this working would seem to further confirm this link.

Also worth noting is Lovecraft's fascination with the zoomorphic transformation between human and batrachian states of being. Frogs and toads appear in various myth-cycles as being sources of wisdom and guidance.

2. Correspondence with others inclined to shamanic work suggests that one of the common positive indicators of animal-spirit possession is changes in visual perception, as well as physiognomic changes.

3. The invocatory techniques were based on drama exercises, some of which can be found in Keith Johnstone's book, *Impro*. The name "Tsathoggua" is very suggestive when trying to move from clear speech to toad-like utterances.

4. This is one of the few occasions that I have used a Mythos entity to effect a direct magical result: healing (admittedly not what one usually associates the Mythos entities with).

If you gaze into the abyss, then the abyss also gazes into you.
— Friedrich Wilhelm Nietzsche

SELECT BIBLIOGRAPHY

Bertiaux, Michael—*The Voudou-Gnostic Workbook* (Magical Childe, 1988)

Borgeaud, Phillipe—*The Cult of Pan in Ancient Greece* (Chicago, 1988)

Burroughs, William S.—*The Place of Dead Roads* (Calder, 1984)

Burroughs, William S.—*The Job* (Calder, 1984)

Carroll, Peter J.—*Liber Null & Psychonaut* (Samuel Weiser, 1987)

Carroll, Peter J.—*Liber Kaos* (Samuel Weiser, 1992)

Carter, L.—*Lovecraft: A Look Behind the Cthulhu Mythos* (Ballantine Books, 1972)

Crowley, Aleister—*The Vision and the Voice* (Sangreal Foundation, 1972)

De Camp, L. S.—*Lovecraft: A Biography* (NEL, 1976)

Falorio, Linda—*The Shadow Tarot* (Headless Press, 1991)

Gleick, James—*Chaos* (Cardinal, 1987)

Grant, Kenneth—*Hecate's Fountain* (Skoob Books, 1993)

Grant, Kenneth—*Nightside of Eden* (Muller, 1972)

Hay, George (ed.)—*The Necronomicon* (Skoob Books, 1992)

Hine, Phil—*Prime Chaos* (Chaos International, 1993)

Linden, Mishlen—*Typhonian Teratomas* (Black Moon, 1991)

Lovecraft, H.P—*The Haunter of the Dark* (Panther, 1965)

Lovecraft, H.P—*At the Mountains of Madness* (Panther, 1970)

Lovecraft, H.P—*Selected Letters Vols. 1–5* (Arkham House, 1965–1971)

Tenebrous, Fra.—*Cults of Cthulhu* (Daath Press, 1987)

Vinci, Leo—*Pan: God of Nature* (Neptune Press, 1993)

Collections

Starry Wisdom—Zebulon, Fra. (ed.) (Pagan News Publications, 1990)

The Nox Anthology—Sennitt & Hewitson-Mays (eds.) (New World Publishing, 1991)

The Starry Wisdom—D.M Mitchell (ed.) (Creation Press, 1994)

Journals

The Pylon, No. 1

Esoterra, No. 2

Nox Magazine, Nos. 3–6

Chaos International, No. 13

Made in the USA
Monee, IL
10 June 2026